Shades of Life

Shades of Life

April D. Williams

authorHOUSE®

AuthorHouse™
1663 Liberty Drive
Bloomington, IN 47403
www.authorhouse.com
Phone: 1-800-839-8640

Published by AuthorHouse   03/18/2013

ISBN: 978-1-4817-3238-3 (sc)
ISBN: 978-1-4817-3237-6 (e)

Library of Congress Control Number: 2013905072

Any people depicted in stock imagery provided by Thinkstock are models, and such images are being used for illustrative purposes only.
Certain stock imagery © Thinkstock.

This book is printed on acid-free paper.

Because of the dynamic nature of the Internet, any web addresses or links contained in this book may have changed since publication and may no longer be valid. The views expressed in this work are solely those of the author and do not necessarily reflect the views of the publisher, and the publisher hereby disclaims any responsibility for them.

Contents

This book is dedicated to the most encouraging and strong woman that I know. When I doubted myself, you were there telling me, "Yes, you can." I thank God for strong, kindhearted women like you. Thank you so much, Velda Virgil.

Special Thanks

Esther Withers

Thoughts in the Shade

I Don't Sing Anymore

My days had long lost their luster.
Dwelling in the shadows, even when there is light,
Drinking water doesn't quench my thirst.
Even when the wind blows, there is no sensation.
Walking for countless days on Mother Earth, I still can't see her
  splendor;
Blades of grass are more capable of rejoicing for their days.
My veins don't race anymore,
My heart, a habitat for grief.
I don't sing anymore.
I blinked only for a moment and lost the purpose,
And now I am gone astray.
Rain on me and penetrate my character.
Breathe on me, so I may live yet again.
Rejuvenate these dry bones.
Weeping in my own obscurity,
Taking refuge in seclusion,
I don't sing anymore.
Oh—now I digress.
The ground shook beneath me,
A wind from the north filled my nostrils.
All that was empty was made whole.
Renewing my strength, mounting wings,
I take my flight into a new dawning.
Vast fields of songs, each caring hope,
I have emerged into a new being,
Taking flight to an endless journey.

I Searched

I have been searching for a long time.
I just couldn't seem to find my place,
Running in a circle for an endless time.
I wondered, *Where's the end to my race?*
Awakening to what seemed to me emptiness,
A void of feelings of being in complete bliss,
It is so cold; nothing but loneliness.
I am fading away each and every day.
I have been searching for a while now.
Is it really that hard to find?
I keep turning around asking—
How can I have a peace of mind?
I am drained of my battling energy,
Collapsing under the weight of the world,
Only bitterness in my heart . . . makes me angry.
Standing still looking into obscurity,
As I lye here dying,
No memories come of good times.
"Damn . . ." I say as I am crying.
I lived without ties or binds;
I had searched only to never find.

Life

All day I feel like I am at the bottom of the barrel.
I walk around nude, refusing to wear my apparel.
My head is always lowered and eyes to the ground,
Looking for zest, which doesn't want to be found.
I move and watch myself from a grave distance
Just to comb my hair; I am fighting resistance.
I don't even want to get up to take a shower;
I feel as if I have climbed a thousand foot tower.
I am always tired.
Something has me by the neck, and I can't breathe.
If it just kills me, that would be the greatest deed.
In my head, I can't even form a decent thought.
In my hands, I hold a bottle of pills I just bought.
The doctor says it would be good for depression.
When did my life enter this stage of regression?
Depression, a disease that brings misery and strife.
I want it back, every vital part of my wonderful life.

This Morning

My eyes opened to a day of uncertainty.
I don't know why, but I hesitate.
Rays of sunlight stream through the window,
Yet an eerie feeling of sadness overwhelms me.
My body feels drained and heavy.
This morning, maybe I will sleep.
It is quiet with a stale calmness.
I fill my lungs with air,
Releasing it with a long sigh.
I stretch my arms toward heaven,
With a deep arch in my back.
This morning, I am not ready for the day,
My muscles tight as I try to stand.
Focusing seems to be a chore,
Small pops as my joints try to align.
My routine is getting too predictable.
I don't want to be bothered today.
This morning . . . sleep will win the day.

Creation

Beyond great divine, near coastlines,
Tranquil and amicable, flowing gently shoreward,
Ruling boldly, powerfully, and infinitely,
Emerges an enormous body of water,
Surging to immense peaks, plummeting to great depths.
Reeling, and rocking, billows flow,
Endless tides turn as a faint wind
Carries a salty aroma.
Cascading waves spraying a mist everywhere
Fade toward the distant shore.
One hears the melodious roar, ever so vaguely,
Of nature's hypnotic creation.

Georgia

Only one place on earth can give me peace of mind.
I yearn to feel the red clay dirt between my toes.
I can smell that sweet aroma from a peach tree—
In the summer is when she shows all her glory.
Me on the porch with my glass of sweet tea,
My rocking chair squeaks as I begin to dream,
But for now, I am far from my country home.
The winds whisper to me, "Daughter, come home."
I still remember the vast fields of honeysuckles
And the endless fields of cotton and corn.
I am staring at the endless blue sky.
In my heart, I long to see her again.
The easy life is what she offers me.
The hustle of the city has grown old.
She offers me fresh air and pecans.
Oh, how I miss her—
Georgia.

Warning

Are we listening to all the signs of the time?
A divine hand came down and disturbed the water,
Taking hundreds of thousands to a watery grave.
A divine foot stomped the earth, causing her to shake,
Causing hundreds of thousands to be buried alive.
From the core of the earth, anger flows from mountaintops.
Ghastly news, a common thing from all around the world.
We are warring with each other, staining the earth with blood.
An entire generation lost from disease, poverty, and neglect.
Road of prosperity grown crooked, narrow, and many suffer.
Our days filled with joy are coming slow, but are still so few.
Are we listening to all the signs of the time?
Have our lives here on Mother Earth come full circle?
Have we done all we can to save ourselves from rapture?
The smell of blood grows thick each day and night.
I search the sky, looking for the white horsemen.
I strain my ears, listening for the trumpets to sound.
So many spew lies, and now many believe in darkness.
The reality is mankind's heart has grown bitter and sour.
We are all now wounded and our doom is looming.
The cries of man will be the only sound after the trumpets.
The smell of burning flesh, the wind will carry for miles.
Are we listening to the signs of the time?

Money

With you, I was never here.
Turn your pockets out, dear.
Tonight, there's no dinner.
You were never a winner.
I am the life of this world.
I rain only on a few.
You say that rent is due,
Your light power gone, and
Phone line is just done.
I am the life of this world.
You wish you had me.
Ain't nothing here free,
Working till hands bleed,
Sowing the earth with seeds,
I am the life of this world.
I am precious like gold.
For me—men sell their souls,
Women will sell their bodies;
All for me—money.

Lies

Lies, lies, and more lies.
Stop telling lies.
All you know are lies.
Let truth breathe sometimes.
Lies, lies, and more lies.
Stop telling lies.
I am sick of your lies.
Let truth breathe sometimes.
Lies, lies, and more lies.
Stop telling lies.
Don't look in my eyes.
Let truth breathe sometimes.
Lies, lies, and more lies.
Stop telling lies.
Get out of my life.
Learn to let truth breathe sometimes.

I Do Not Understand

We are a people who have carried the weight of the world.
There are no other people like our people on this earth.
We are the cradle of civilization.
We have endured much over the centuries,
But we remained a resilient and visual people.
The blood of kings and queens runs through our veins.
My brothers,
I do not understand why the corner over education.
I do not understand why a cage over freedom.
I do not understand sagging pants over dignity.
I do not understand the lack of responsibility.
There was a time you stood tall and anchored the family.
From the brows of our ancestors, you built this country.
Now you roam as if in the desolate desert.
We are waiting for your return to your rightful place.
Now I say to my sisters,

Our big momma always taught us about lion strength.
We are the preservers of a potent race.
Our children look to us for that audacity to hope.
So many of us alone to carry out this task.
They see when we compromise ourselves.
I do not understand why we don't take the time to pamper ourselves.
I do not understand why our lips drip with anger.
I do not understand why it's hard to say, "love you," and myself.
I do not understand why the same mistakes again and again.
I say to my brothers and sisters:
We must strive to break the chain of poverty.
We have to put aside our differences.
If we do not lead our children, then who will?
It is time for us to march together to the same rhythm.
Why is this so difficult?
I do not understand so much.

Why Hate?

My race doesn't define who I am.
"I am just a number," says Uncle Sam.
I might be a blue or a Democrat;
You might be a red or aristocrat.
I might enjoy the game of football;
You might like hitting that white ball.
I might be the poorest of the poor;
You got money, still looking for more.
We are different, so why hate?
I don't dot all my i's and cross my t's,
Unlike you, with stature and pedigrees.
The car I drive may be twenty years old;
For you, a Rolls Royce trimmed in gold.
I have a roof and four walls I call home;
You have a mansion with a golden dome.
I am not rich, but I am working for my keep;
No money worries, and you don't lose sleep.
We are different, so why hate?

What's the Difference?

How many of us take something to the afterlife?
Yet we fight over land that doesn't belong to us,
Drawing lines in the sand and saying, "This is mine."
You don't realize it has been here millions of years.
We have different religious beliefs and practices:
Atheist, Christians, Buddhism, Hinduism and Muslim.
Even if you don't believe in God, you believe in that
Caucasoid, Mongoloid, and Negroid, all the same race.
Yet we spill blood because we don't have the same face.
What's the difference?
All of our time here on earth is limited, a grave for us all.
We all return to our fragile state of being, dust or ashes.
Yet we just can't seem to get along with each other.
You, Democrat, Communist, Republican, and Socialist.
Forget you and the party that you associate with.
I will not be enslaved to your ideology that's forgotten.
We have to work for the greater good of mankind.
If you bleed, then I bleed, and when you cry, I cry.
Our lives are to be treasured, not consumed with warring.
We are all citizens of Mother Earth. Open your eyes.
Tell me what's the difference?

A Miracle Just for Me

When I was only a child,
I dreamed the impossible.
I even wished upon a star,
Hoping my dreams would come alive.
Or would that all fade away,
Leaving me to fight another day?
It's all so amazing to me,
That I only had to believe.

Here I am in the mist of it all,
The greatest moment of all.
It might have seemed impossible,
But anything in life is possible,
More than I could ever dream,
A miracle just for me.

Going through trial after trial,
I would have run a million miles,
Crawled the valley lows,
For this one moment in time.
I spent my life chasing a dream.
Now my dream has captured me.
It's been a long, long road,
And I finally reached my goal.

Seasons of Love
in the Shade

I Am In Love

I am in love with a man,
A man that ain't even mine.
I am doing all I can
To keep him off my mind.
Sitting here in the dark
With my hand on the phone,
Wondering, *Why did we start?*
Now I am feeling all alone.
I am in love with a man,
A man that ain't even mine.
I am doing all I can
To keep him off my mind.
I wish I could say
That I feel good, y'all.
But that just ain't today.
I am feeling so small.
I am in love with a man,
A man that ain't even mine.

I am doing all I can
To keep him off my mind.
I saw them the other day, y'all.
She gave an easy smile
As they walked through the mall.
It hurt me for a while.
I am in love with a man,
A man that ain't even mine.
I am doing all I can
To keep him off my mind.
I can't live this way,
So I had to let him go.
I keep reliving that day.
He don't come around no mo'.
I am still in love with a man,
A man that ain't even mine.
I am doing all that I can
To keep him off my mind.

Your Husband, My Sweet Daddy-Man

He might be your husband,
But he is my sweet daddy-man.
You might have the ring.
My gifts he will always bring.
A piece of paper gives you claim.
He comes to me, there's no shame.
He might be your husband,
But he is my sweet daddy-man.
I am the other woman in his life.
My purpose is not to bring strife.
I fulfill his fantasies, and that's all.
Don't worry because I never call.
He might be your husband,
But he is my sweet daddy-man.
I got bills, and he's got the money.
Cash is what I want, honey.
A home wrecker wants to steal.
Manwhores, girl I know the deal.
He might be your husband,
But he is my sweet daddy-man.
He loves you, but devoted he's not.
Call me that word . . . I get that a lot.
He might be your husband,
But he's my sweet daddy man.

My purpose is to give him a thrill.
Five years. Can you handle that pill?
You say you followed him in the car.
This instant is going to leave a scar.
He might be your husband,
But he is my sweet daddy-man.
You say you want to know why.
Because he can, and that's no lie.
If it wasn't me, then another will be.
So it might as well be me.
He might be your husband,
But he is my sweet daddy-man.
I am sorry for the tears you cry.
So many have the same lullaby.
My heart is not made of stone.
You want me to leave him alone.
He might be your husband,
But he is my sweet daddy-man.
Trust me when I say I am no threat.
I might be the one to live in regret.
My life filled with stolen moments,
Treated like Christmas ornaments.
He might be your husband,
But he is my sweet daddy-man.

Breakfast

This morning I seemed to float to the kitchen.
My quart-sized pot steaming with cheese grits,
And my smoked Georgia sausage in the oven
With my buttermilk biscuits on top.
I am waiting to start my eggs last.
Then it happened . . .
He walked up behind me and caressed me so gently,
Then he kissed me on the side of my neck.
Tiny sensations of passion roamed throughout.
I opened my mouth to release a moan from deep within.
Memories of the moments of complete bliss emerged.
I smell him, and I can feel him through my robe.
My senses are reeling, and my heart is beating swiftly.
His hands moving feverishly over the frame of my body.
He spins me around and kisses me urgently.
I struggle to regain my composure . . . and I say,
"What about breakfast?
He says, "I am having what I want."

What Happened to Me?

I have been running for a long time,
Concrete in my heart for a lifetime,
My eyes piercing without feelings,
Many harsh words to keep you reeling.
What happened to me?
One morning, it was like spring,
Sparrow outside my window singing,
Hairs on my neck standing at attention,
A glowing sensation not to mention.
What happened to me?
My inner being stomping in a dance,
Not recognizing myself at first glance.
Who is the woman that's just beaming,
Her eyes full of life and gleaming?
What happened to me?
I really did not believe in it at all.
How dare you break down my walls?
It is not my bleeping will.
I am starting to feel a chill.
What happened to me . . . Love!

Scared

I can't say it yet, baby.
I don't know if I am.
I have been burnt.
I am so scared.
     Baby, I breathe you.
     I throw rose petals,
     Celebrating love for you.
     Don't be scared.
You are so sure, boy.
I am still hesitating.
My heart skips a beat.
I am so scared.
     If you only trust me, girl,
     We'll go to the mountaintop.
     I'll carry you through valley lows.
     Don't be scared.
I'll give my heart, boy,
Taking a chance on love.
I see your beautiful spirit,
Though I am still scared.

Not Your Day

I was happy to be starting a new life
With a man who took me as his wife.
Beaming with the joy that I found,
I ran into you finding my way around.
You came across as someone to trust,
Someone I had no reason to mistrust.
       Happy to have a new friend and all,
       But you were setting me up for a fall.
       You told yourself you could be better,
       But I know my man to the letter.
       I know all about loneliness.
       It can fill the heart with sadness.
But never forget your respectability.
In the end, it will be about accountability.
Look at you, standing there, looking a fool.
I won't slap you because I can play it cool.
You see this gold band? I put it on his hand.
You had your little plan to steal my man.
       Today ain't the day.
       You'd better be on your way.
       My man is a good man.
       He loves me, you understand?
       You lose when it comes to my man

I Ain't Leaving

I am so sorry for every lie that I told.
I was the one cheating, being so bold.
You felt like a rising star in the night.
I fought the urge with all my might.
My indiscretion is causing you pain,
But I ain't leaving my wife.
What we shared was a moment.
I see in your eyes the torment.
I am so ashamed of my weakness.
I know you stand now in bleakness.
I pretended to be someone I'm not.
Now you threaten to tell my wife.
I ain't leaving.
You say you will send dirty photos.
I didn't mean to hurt you, heaven knows.
You say you will call all times of the night.
You'll try to hurt me with all of your might.
I am sorry for all the heartache I've caused,
But I ain't leaving my wife.

No Words

I saw my sister yesterday.
She was battered and bruised.
Her eye blackened, and
Her lip split, dried with blood.
She dropped her head in shame.
I say to her, "Leave him."
She offered me no words.
I asked, "Why stay?"
My heart filled with sorrow.
I don't know about tomorrow.
"Is it because you don't want to be alone?
Is it because you love him?"
She offered me no words.
"You deserve better," I said.
She opened her mouth and said,
"Leave."

Gold Digger

When we are born, we don't know the past.
We live by example, things taught to us.
So many of us are born into poverty.
We see the life of our mother who struggles,
So we dare to dream of a better life for ourselves.
We want good fathers for our children.
Does this make me a gold digger?
I want a man who earns his keep,
A strong man who can love me,
And I am not bitter.
I just want us to do better.
You will not mistreat me.
The blood of kings and queens is in my veins.
Who is a gold digger?
I was made for you and you for me.
I am glad you have found your footing.
You made us all so very proud.
I was there when you had nothing.

We walked through the struggle together.
I was told there are no shining knights in the ghetto,
So I must be a gold digger.
You stand there in your fine suit.
Memories of me you just won't keep,
Leaving me behind like some dirty secret.
Truth is, nobody knows you better than me.
You will not tell me what I don't deserve.
Diamonds and gold don't have meaning.
But you label me "gold digger."
There ain't enough money in world
To make me think less of myself.
We are preservers of a potent race.
We pass down to our children the audacity to hope.
This, my brother, is what you just don't know.
The only thing I am guilty of is loving my brother.

You Ain't No Dog

It's my job to bathe him,
My duty to feed him.
We go on long walks.
He has no words to talk,
Yet he knows of who I am.
He shows appreciation every day.
But you, the one man that I love,
So often, you take advantage of my love.
I make sure that I feed you.
I make sure to listen to you.
When you don't come home, I am hurt.
You aint' no dog.
My dog is loyal because I take care of him.
A dog can run off on a whim.
He can stray as far as the next state,
Leaving me to wonder about his fate,
But he never stops trying to find his way.
You ain't no dog.
You break my heart time and time again.
I realize now that I can't win,
Drained by this tired relationship.
I'm gonna just jump this old ship.
My dog loves me.
And you ain't no dog.

Still Sneakin'

For a mighty long time,
I tried to figure out
What went wrong.
I searched my heart.
The only answer I found—
You just didn't love me.
>   I washed your clothes,
>   Cooked your food.
>   I braided your hair,
>   Treated you like a king.
>   You still went sneakin'.
Dealt with babies' mommas
When you were low on cash.
I gave you all I had.
When you didn't have a job,
I tried so hard to lift you up,
You uninspiring man.
>   I washed your clothes,
>   Cooked your food,
>   I braided your hair,
>   Treated you like a king.
>   You still went sneakin'.
Once a cheat, always a cheat,
Not deserving a second chance.
But your tears kept me around.
This time, you won't get a glance.
I have to say, "Get to steppin'
'Cause you still sneakin'."

All I Wanted

He said I work hard to support my family.
Day after day, she beats me down with her words.
I can't take this much longer. I thought I was stronger.
She grinded me down until I was two feet tall,
My manhood just flat out insulted.
I am not the kind to raise my hand,
But she provokes me, and so I walk away.
All I ever wanted was a happy home.
Her fists she pounds into my back,
Her anger unleashed in a violent rage.
I try to stay for my kids' sake,
But I am lonely, and she is not content.
So today, I will just fly away.
She won't have me to knock around.
Her words cut me like stones.
All I ever wanted was a happy home.

The Love of my Life

My baby called yesterday.
She's coming home today.
I couldn't sleep last night.
I want things to be just right.
She is the apple of my eye.
Without her, I will surely die.
This is a love that won't fade.
Planning the best way to say,
>"You are the love of my life.
>You are going to be my wife.
>You make me a better man.
>Without you, I can't stand."

Then a knock on the door,
Telling me my baby is no more.
She was just twenty miles away.
There are no words I can say.
Please tell me it's not true.
All I ever wanted was you, and
This diamond for your hand.
>You made me a better man.
>You are the love of my life.
>You are going to be my wife.
>You made me a better man.
>Without you, I can't stand.

Two Years Too Late
I was so in love with you.
That is why it hurts so bad.
You cut me, that's true.
I gave you all that I had.
You left without a word.
My love meant nothing,
The whole thing absurd.
Leave a note or something.
You could have opened up
And told me your feelings,
Like adults with tea cups.
Now we have no dealings.
You are two years too late.
I have gone on with my life,
One hundred weeks to date.
You brought misery and strife.
You are two years too late.

I Don't Want You Anymore

You know I put my best foot forward.
I loved with every ounce of my soul.
Reeling in the death our relationship,
To put it simply: I don't want you anymore.
I lay next to you, feeling so abandoned.
We have shared so much over the years.
I had not heard the words I needed to hear.
I don't want you anymore.
My heart shattered in a million pieces.
Maybe you don't care enough to say it.
All I ever wanted was to be loved by you.
I don't want you anymore.
Now you don't even offer, "I am sorry."
I blinded myself to your philandering ways.
Oh—then you got too comfortable.
I don't want you anymore.
Maybe one day you will come to realize
That I would have loved you for a lifetime.
I am leaving now and only yourself to blame.
I don't want you anymore.

Mournful in the Shade

Father to Son

When he was a child, he would just beam.
He followed his old man, wanting to know things.
I was so proud when he chose to serve.
I wanted him to have everything he deserved.
My son was a great solider.
I tried to teach him everything I knew.
Men like him are still so few.
Now I stand and salute you,
Caressing the red, white, and blue.
My son was a great soldier.
"Amazing Grace" carried on the wind.
You will live in my heart, never to end.
A hero has returned home.
My spirit for life lost, to forever roam.
My son was a great soldier.

Tired of War

I will never forget the fight,
It may be brutal with no end in sight,
The blood flowing from my veins,
Flowing from my enemies veins.
Free will, I am told is the cause.
My finger on trigger without pause.
I refuse to die today.
I have come not to stay,
Hoping you see things my way.
Casualties of war are on my mind,
But I keep moving, not to be left behind.
It is like second nature to take a man's life.
My days are filled with misery and strife.
I long to walk the peaceful shores.
I don't want to study war no more.
Maybe death will come for me today.
That is peace, in a way.
So will it come for me today?

Crying Sun

I am in a foreign land,
With weapon in hand,
Under the scorching sun.
She seldom gets to glimpse her son,
Her mild-mannered moonchild.
He yields to her . . . the crying sun.
> I roam this enormous wasteland,
> Giving myself to the task at hand.
> Her rays searing against my skin.
> Oh, I know how she misses her kin.
> Great mercy I begged her today.
> Only sizzling tears from the crying sun.
She bears witness of mankind's cruelness,
No place in the world without harshness.
She sets with a frown and rises with the same.
"Ashes," she says, "from which you all came."
Body drenched in sweat and my enemy near.
All the while, she is observing . . . the crying sun.
> When she is away, her son brings bleakness.
> He rages sometimes with an awesome fierceness.
> Desert winds and sands scorch just like his mother.
> My comrades stay close and huddle together.
> I am not indigenous to this land but—
> Tomorrow she will reign again . . . the crying sun.

Shadows of the Mountain

It was an awful day when they came down.
An attack on American soil was the cause.
Now I hug this mountain to end it all.
You, a coward who will never face his enemy.
There is no honor in a hidden warrior.
Your face grey from fear and words weak,
You who dare not stare in my eyes.
I am an American soldier. I run toward you.
Come out and face me like a man.
Now I wait for you in the shadows of the mountain.

Breeding Suicide

They have the faces of angels.
You look into their eyes and
Only see the innocence.
A mural of bright colors
Is what they are told awaits
Them on other side.
Children who are orphaned
And abandoned and can't
Provide for themselves.
They are not able to decide
What is right and wrong at this
Age.
They are raised here for years,
Brain washed into committing
Suicide.
I loathe the ones who
Have robbed them of a life that
Could have been.
They breed them so the war
Will have no end, and innocent
People will continue to die.

If I See One

If I see one, he is just dead.
He covers himself from
The top of his head
To the bottom of his feet.
If I see one, he is just dead.
More often than not,
He will bring great
Destruction from under his
Apparel.
If I see one, he is just dead.
I don't have time to waste.
He will shed the blood
Of many innocents just to
Kill one.
If I see one, he is just dead.

Blood on the Sand

I was walking through this desert,
Then that is when I found it.
The stench was overwhelming,
The scenery gruesome:
An area, blood of something.
I walked closer and finally
Saw what it was.
A foot with a sandal and
Nothing else more.
My stomach churned as it
Smelled something awful.
Did it belong to my enemy
Or was it of an innocent?
There is no way to tell,
So I dig a hole to bury
The lone part.
Blood on the sand.
No one offered any words.
So I muttered, "Rest in peace."
Then I picked up my rifle,
And away we went.

Mourn for the Dead

I killed four men today,
Men with no faces.
Their comrades won't come
Back to carry them home.
So I will dig through the waves
Of heavy sand, and I will pay
Tribute to them for their families.
I am only human, and I will mourn
For the dead.
I am in a war, the war is not in me.
Yes, I have a cause, but at this point,
I am not sure of the outcome.
I will serve my country with my
Last breath and push forward until
The chief says, "Time to come home."
So I fight the men with no faces.
I am only human, and I will mourn
For the dead.

Take Me Home

I am a captive of war.
No secrets will I tell.
My end comes soon.
My enemy has no name.
I no longer have a name.
There is no fear in my heart.
I say to him, "Leave me."
      Now bleeding from wounds,
      My captor amused by it all,
      But my spirit did not break.
      I am an American soldier.
      My roots lie in the heartlands.
      I have walked the shores of Florida.
      I say to him, "Leave me,"
So my comrades may find me.
To die in this country, not my wish.
I have a home, and she is beautiful.
I am dreaming of America,
The land where I was born free.
I say to him, "Leave me,"
So my comrades can take me home.

Mother to Daughter

I knew you before you knew who you were.
We listened to classical music and read.
The day you were born brought me joy.
Your first steps I remember like yesterday.
I'll carry you in my spirit.
You blossomed into a beautiful woman.
I lifted you up when you chose to serve.
It takes a mighty woman to sacrifice her life,
So that others may live in freedom.
I'll carry you in my spirit.
As I stand here, holding our American flag,
Precious memories I'll hold in my heart.
An eagle soars high across the vast sky,
Reminding me of your great courage.
I'll carry you in my spirit.

Going Home

As I look at the vast ocean of sand,
My mind admires its beauty from above.
My heart knows the danger that it brings.
The searing sun upon my skin, a reminder
I have thirsted many days on this land.
I have been cut by coldness of night.
Now is the time for jubilation.
I am returning home to my first love.
She awaits me with open arms, full of love.
I have missed her with every fiber of my being.
This land cannot compare to her of whom I long.
This war is ending for me, and I mourn my comrades.
We did not leave any behind, though they died.
They made the trip home, and I grieve for them.
Now it is my time, and I am going home.

Adoration in the Shade

Here I Am

The angels had met me at the end of my journey.
They opened their arms, and I was not afraid.
I was carried on the four winds,
And I have arrived at the perfect resting place.
I was with you for a while.
Here I am.
Now I have roamed far from my home,
And I am in an unfamiliar place, but welcomed.
I am missing your faces, but I am not alone.
They have brought me to a city of joy.
My spirit is rejoicing.
Here I am.
My feet carried me swiftly to the golden strait.
My name has been called.
My father has a glorious crown.
I have returned to an everlasting life.
With him, I shall reign.
Here I am.
There are no raging waters, only peaceful tides.
Just keep on living, and I will live through you.
Now I am in the bosom of my Lord.
My soul dances in victory.
I shall rest until we all meet again.

Ode to a Good Man

*F or it was in one of the darkest hours of my life when the peaceful
waters were raging tides.*

*L ife, for me, had come to a sudden halt, and the mountains had
blocked my view.*

*E ven though it seemed that hope was lost, and I was surrounded
by sickness, I was saved; but who would have thought God would
send a ram?*

*M y heart leaped with joy—a true man of honor and valor rose
from above the waters, and hope was restored in my life.*

*I t is one the greatest moments of kindness ever to be witnessed on
this side of creation;*

*N ow the time has come, and the tides have shifted. The wind has
changed directions. May*

*G od's goodness and mercy follow you all the days of your life, and
I will always be grateful for your generosity.*

Grandaddy

Though the sun has set on your brow for the last time,
My heart is heavy; I am no longer privileged with your presence.
Countless days of our freedom to love one another,
A distinguished love from a distinguished gentleman.
I've always known the hero that lies in you.
Your words often made for laughter. I remember the joy.
A strong man to guide children to the pathway of life.
A dedicated man to whatever his heart desired.
Even though my heart is heavy with sorrow,
I've always known the hero that lies in you,
A last of his kind.
An aroma of a cigar comes to mind.
The jollies of laughter make me smile.
In my younger years, you stood ten feet tall.
I've always known the hero that lies in you.
At that appointed hour, you took flight
Into a brand new dawning of an everlasting peace.
Take refuge in an awesome serenity.
Sleep on, grandaddy—just know
I've always known the hero that lies in you.

Go Tell the People

We have another changeling.
"A new one," you say.
Oh, what a glorious day!
More hope for us on the way.
Go tell the people,
"A Nubian king is soon to be revealed."
Prepare the rose petals,
Sound the trumpets,
All dancers come near.
Go tell the people,
"Our prince has crossed a new threshold."
He is no longer child, but a young man,
Bringing with him every prospect to be had.
Go tell the people,
"He is here! He is here!"
We welcome you, Your Grace.
His lifts his voice with words to say,
"I carry peace in my heart for the nation."
Go tell the people.

In My Soul

Down in my soul cries, "Glory!"
We are glad, and this is the day.
Our hearts and minds belong to you, Lord.
We thank you for your many blessings.
Down in my soul cries, "Glory!"
We can see where you brought us from.
You took us and molded us,
And we step out of your lab of redemption.
Look at what the ALL POWERFUL has done.
He has provided for us.
Down in my soul cries, "Glory!"
He helped us through hard times.
The struggle was great, but
Look at us now.
Mountains have crumbled because of the blood.
Down in my soul cries, "Glory!"

Lord, you gave me a virtuous woman.
She has been my pillar of hope.
She has given me encouragement.
She takes care of me.
She holds me close to her bosom.
Down in my soul cries, "Glory!"
Lord, you have given me a holy man.
He teaches me in your way.
He takes care of me.
He is my jewel, and he has my heart.
Down in my soul cries, "Glory!"
We thank you for giving us each other.
We feel your blessing.
Our love is strong, and with you, it's stronger.
Down in our soul cries, "Glory!"

A House for His Name

We have toiled in the vineyard a long time,
Working for the greater good of mankind.
Now we see that it wasn't done in vain,
We held the word close, our loyalty maintained.
It was only by his grace,
He has saw fit to bring us to this place
Where we not only sing,
But we shout.
We play tambourines.
My God, we cry out.
A house for his name.
Though the winds blew and billows raged,
"Hallelujah," we shouted in the highest praise.
The journey filled with days of weakness,
But in the end, we offered up our best.
It was only by his grace,
He has saw fit to bring us to this place
Where we not only sing,
But we shout.

We play tambourines.
My God, we cry out.
A house for his name.
Because we were faithful over a few things.
God poured us out many blessings.
We come forth with a new dance.
We will lift him up at every chance.
It was only by his grace,
He has saw fit to bring us to this place
Where we not only sing,
But we shout.
We play tambourines.
My God, we cry out.
A house for his name.
In Jesus's name,
In Jesus's name,
A house for his name.
My God, a house for his name!

Backslider

When I started my race,
I became aware of your grace.
My eyes were open to see
Things were not the same for me.
I felt love in your company.
Eager was I to study the word,
Shouting and dancing in freedom,
Working for a seat in the kingdom.
Then unknown to me, it happened.
An unfulfilled spirit blossomed.
I lost my song that was in my soul,
Standing in obscurity, no light to behold.
I don't hear my Lord's voice anymore.
Now I am wandering in a desolate desert,
My throat so parched I can't cry out.
He doesn't want me anymore, no doubt.
I am neck deep in my original sin,
My soul corrupted with wickedness.
I can't find my mustard seed.
I am a backslider.

That Awful Day

I awoke this morning with a terrible fright.
I wasn't able to hear, see, or speak.
My heart heavy was with grief, and it wasn't right.
I tried to move my limbs and was weak.
Then, a voice spoke to my soul:
"You ran a long time trying to reach your goal,
Your life of one who circled in the desert.
You stopped sending your timber up to heaven."
A gift of song, but lifting him, you would advert
Your entire life force, stained and now taken,
A child who had forgotten the master's will.
Death was upon you, like a thief creeping in the night,
To be caught with your work undone—a bitter pill.
That awful day has come, and he cast you from his sight.

Wading in the Water

This is my day of salvation.
My spirit is leaping in joy.
Soul was dead of starvation.
My wicked ways I did enjoy,
Living life the way I wanted.
No master I sought to obey.
Things I've done now haunted
My soul for Satan; I say, "Nay."
These dry bones live yet again,
Waters of redemption upon me.
Deliverance, I am free from sin.
His plan made plain so I can see.
My hands and feet brand new.
My soul has been washed in the blood.
A new being that he always knew,
As I am wading in the water.

Thank You

I have been astray too long, Father.
There are no excuses for me to offer.
Day in and out, I had the use of my mind,
Yet I robbed you by not offering my time.
Thank You.
Thank you for guiding and holding me.
You didn't have to do it and glory to be.
I stand now, clapping and stomping in joy.
Fallen, you picked me up. I count it all joy.
Thank You.
Thank you for not killing me while in my sin.
I have been led by your Holy Spirit once again.
You said that all I needed was a little more faith.
This is the day the Lord has made. "Be glad," I say.
Thank You.

Thank You So Much!

About the Author

April Williams was born in Bainbridge, Georgia, in August of 1974. She was the fourth child born to her mother, a fieldworker, and father, a brick mason. When she was just a toddler, her mother relocated the family to Florida and settled in the all-American city of South Miami. April attended all the local schools, including Miami-Dade Community College.

April was an active volunteer in her community. For years she worked on programs, including the Dr. Martin Luther King Jr. Annual Celebrations and many South Miami Community Outreach Gospel Programs. Along with her writing, singing has always been a passion of hers. She was one of the founding members of the Miracle Voice Ensemble.

Many years ago, her pen was her way of escaping some of the hard times she faced. She discovered that she could live victoriously and help others by writing about her experiences, triumphs, and pains. She brought us her first novel, *I Don't Sing Anymore*. April's writing brings concrete reality to the issues within the twenty-first century world. Now she invites us to read her new poetry, *Shades of Life*. She exhorts and motivates her readers to remain constant and dedicated to their passions.

About the Book

Shades of Life talks about four different seasons of life. The author speaks on life, love, war, and worship. Many human emotions are brought forth in a prolific and raw way.